THE Kids' Worker's CLIP ART BOOK

COMPILED BY SHERYL HAYSTEAD

Featuring the art of: *Rick Bundschuh, Curt Dawson, Tom Finley, Dennis Jones, Catherine Leary, Jim Padgett, Bron Smith, Joyce Thimsen, Chris Wilson and Chizuko Yasuda.*

HOW TO MAKE CLEAN COPIES FROM THIS BOOK.

You may make copies of portions of this book with a clean conscience if:

- you (or someone in your organization) are the original purchaser.
- you are using the copies you make for a noncommercial purpose (such as teaching or promoting a ministry) within your church or organization.
- you follow the instructions provided in this book.

However, it is illegal for you to make copies if:

- you are using the material to promote, advertise or sell a product or service other than for ministry fundraising.
- you are using the material in or on a product for sale.
- you or your organization are **not** the original purchaser of this book.

By following these guidelines you help us keep our products affordable. Thank you.

Gospel Light

CONTENTS

FUN
page!

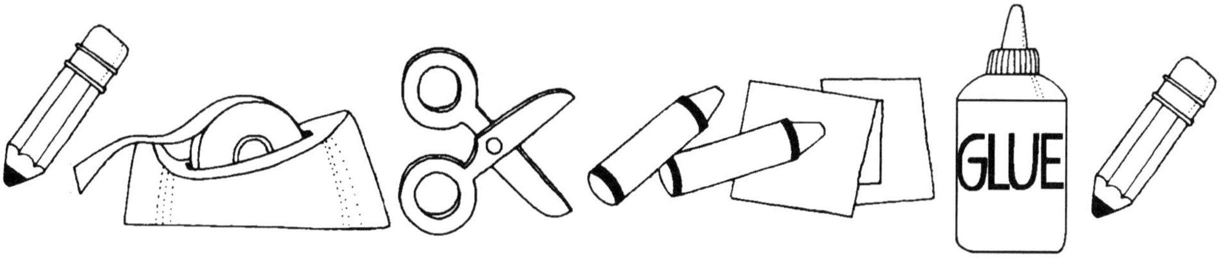

HOW TO USE THIS BOOK

Collect These Tools and Supplies:

→ Photocopy machine and paper

→ Transparent tape, rubber cement or glue stick

→ Scissors

OPTIONAL:
→ Typewriter and paper

Follow These Easy Steps:

1. Cut out the artwork and copy. You may want to enlarge or reduce artwork and/or copy if you have access to a photocopier with that capability. Optional: Type additional copy on a piece of white paper.

2. Decide where to position the art and your copy. Either make a few pencil sketches on scratch paper or decide in your mind the basic arrangement you will use. Plan to leave a one-half inch (or more) margin on your paper.

3. Tape, glue or use rubber cement to attach the artwork and all copy to a sheet of white paper. (Lines may be caused by the edges of paper you've glued to your final copy. Prevent lines by taping all edges.)

4. Make as many copies as you need.

CHILDREN

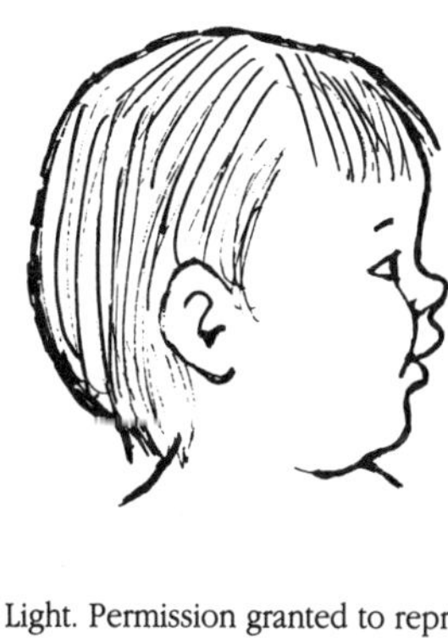

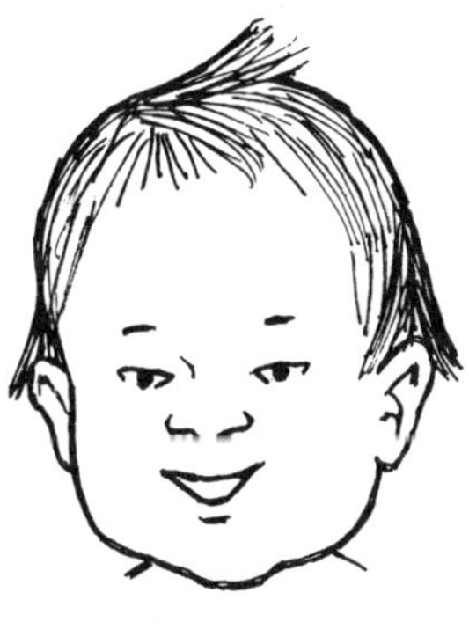

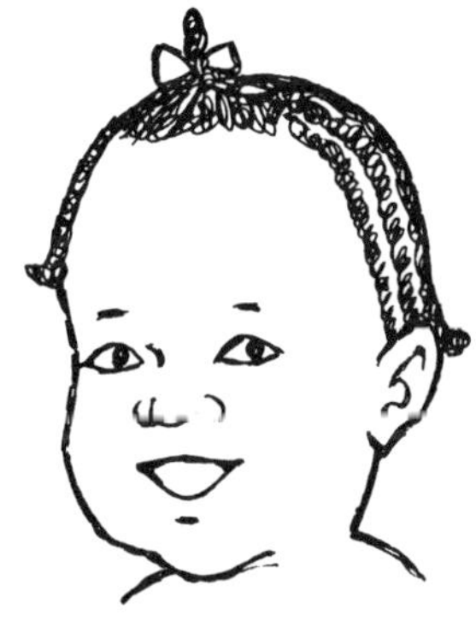

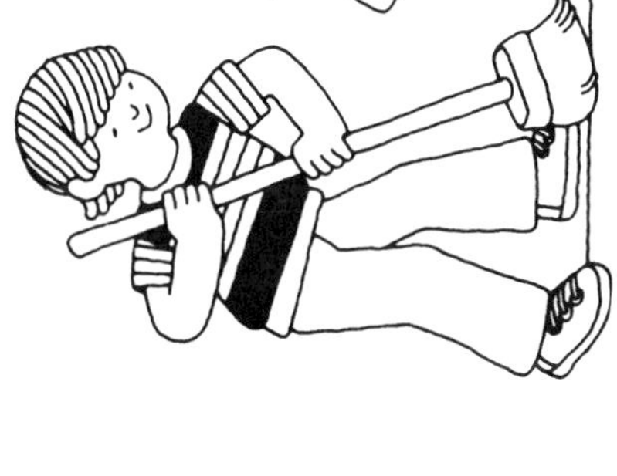

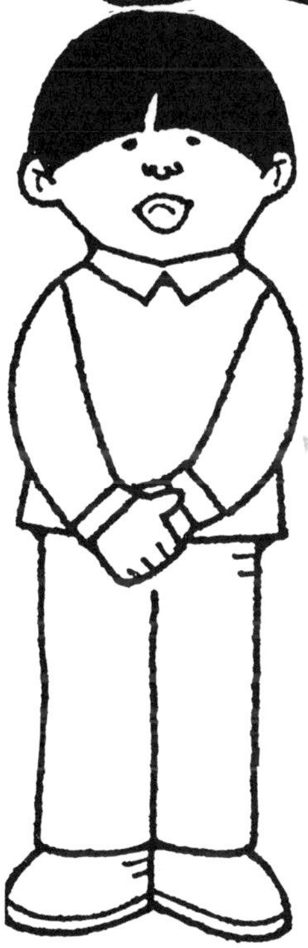

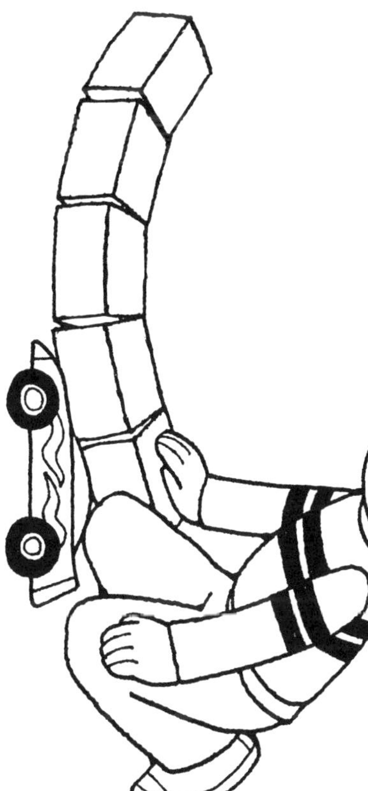

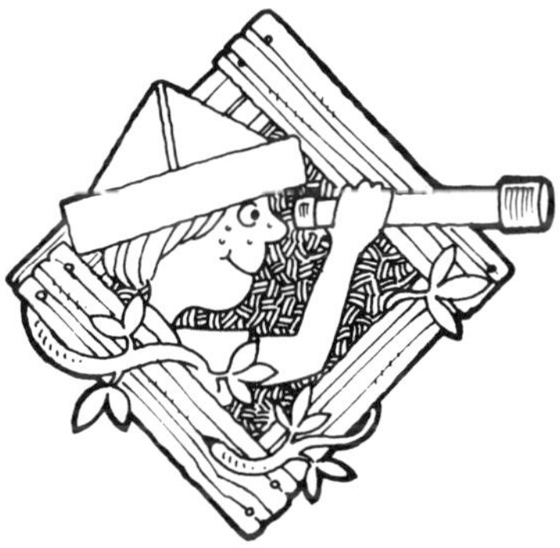

Surf

Surf

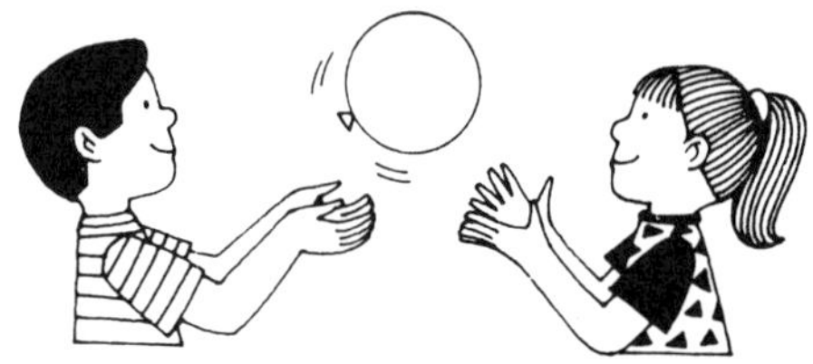

FAMILIES

SEASONS

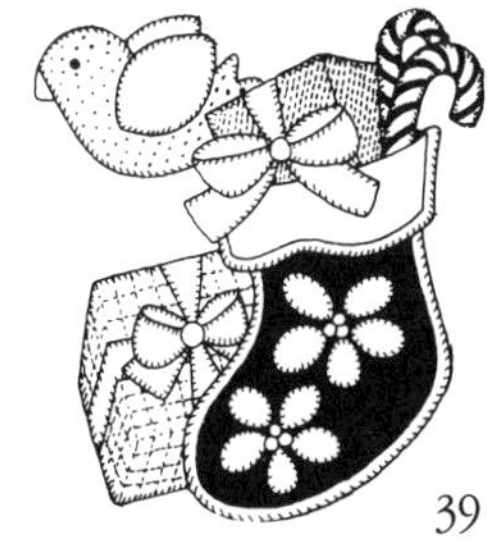

Love!

Love!

ALLELUIA!

ALLELUIA!

ALLELUIA
ALLELUIA

Summer!

Summer!

BIBLE STUDY

BIBLE

THE BIBLE

THE BIBLE

THE BIBLE

BIBLE
Tools

BIBLE
Tools

GOD'S WORD
MAKE IT A DAILY HABIT!

GOD'S WORD
MAKE IT A DAILY HABIT!

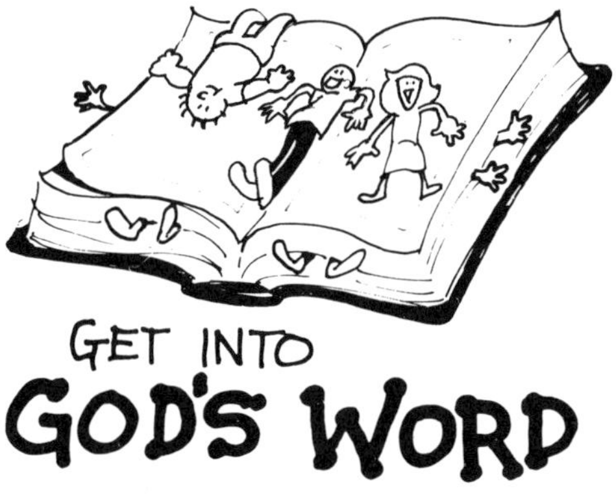
GET INTO
GOD'S WORD

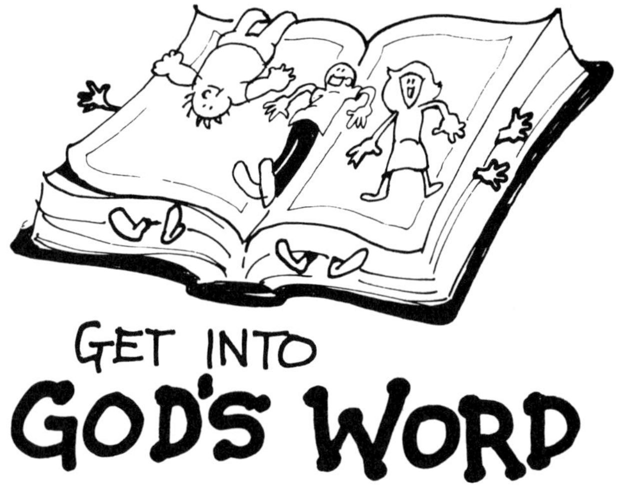
GET INTO
GOD'S WORD

BIBLE

BIBLE

BIBLE

GOD'S
WORD

BIBLE

BIBLE

GOD'S
WORD

GOD'S
WORD

HOLY
BIBLE

BIBLE

BIBLE

BIBLE

BIBLE

MUSIC

STRUM!

STRUM!

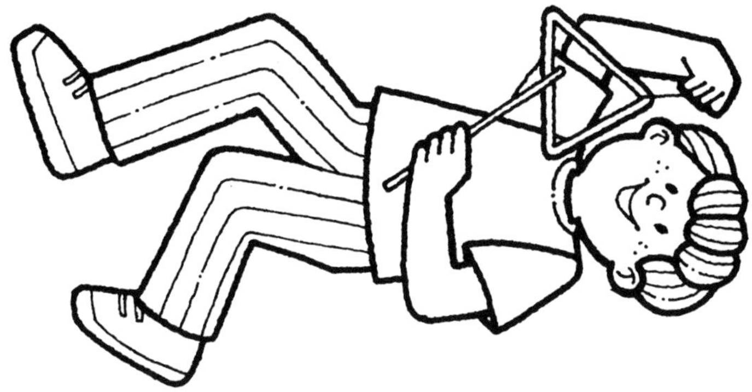

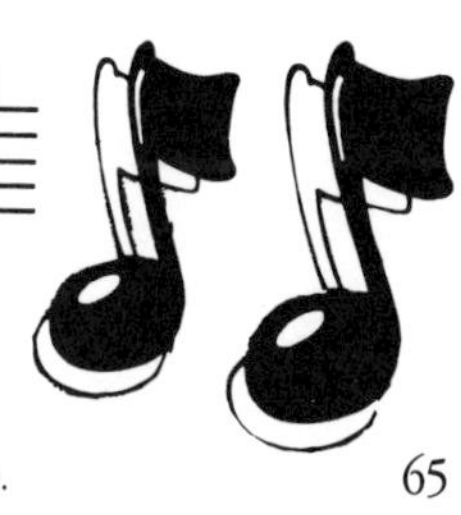

ANIMALS

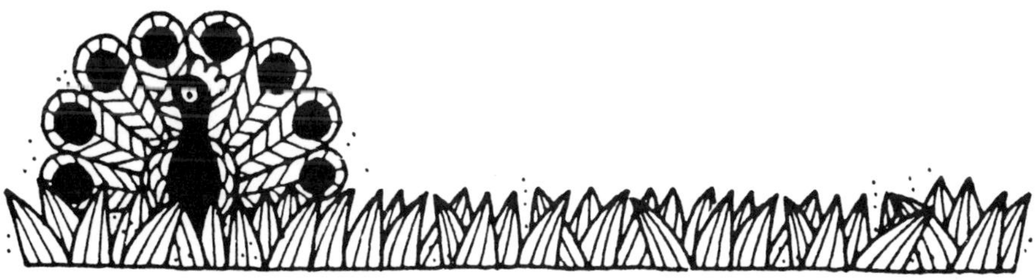

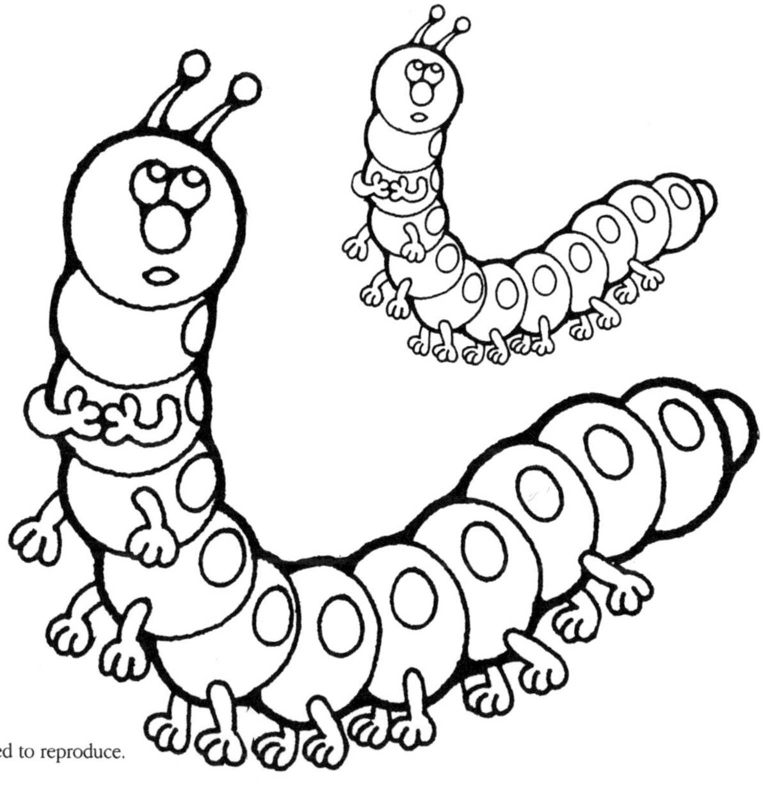

NATURE

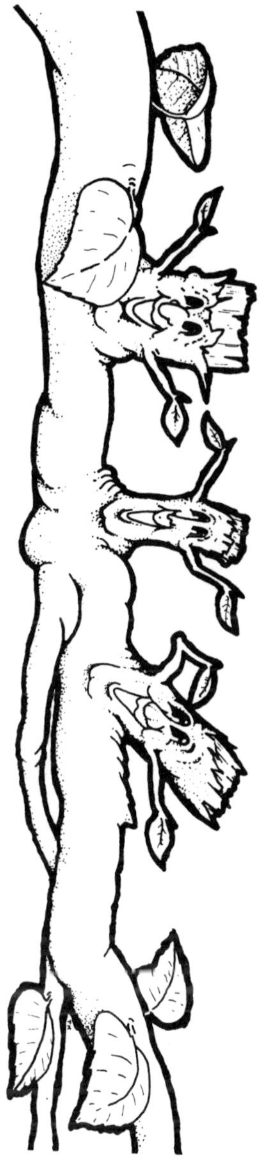

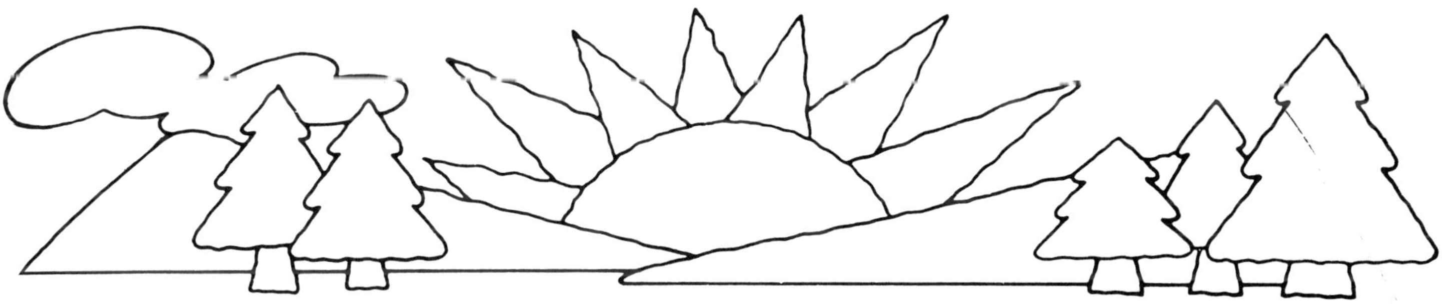

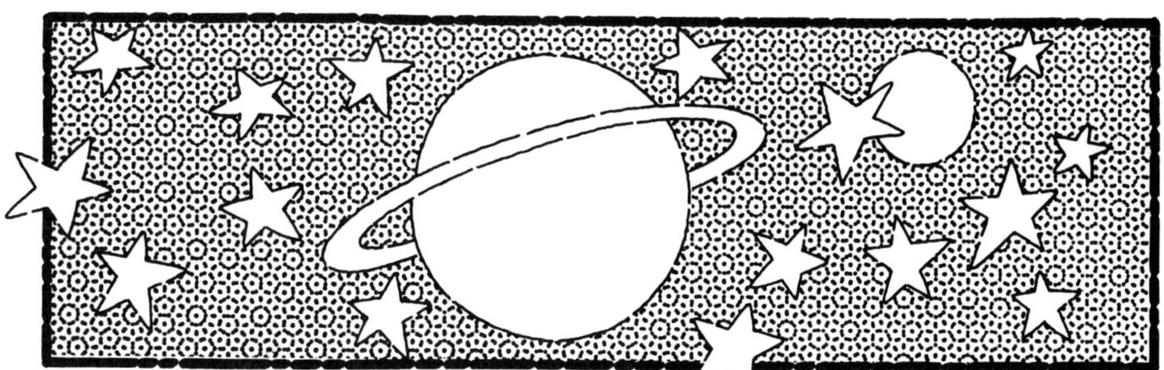

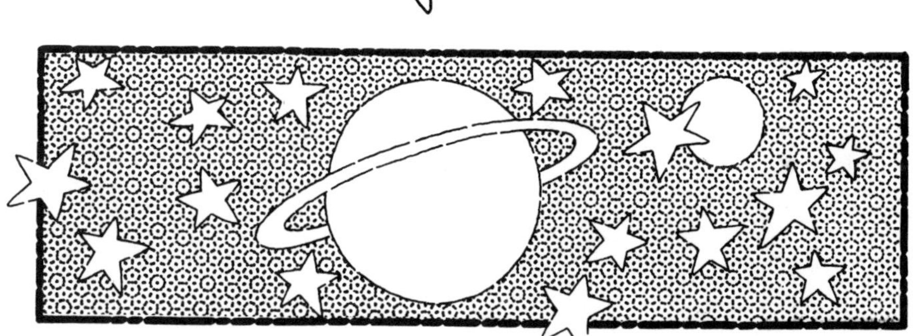

SPECIAL EVENTS

BBQ

Big Picnic!

Bike Hike

Big Picnic!

Bike Hike

MOUNTAIN MANIA

MOUNTAIN MANIA

BOWLING

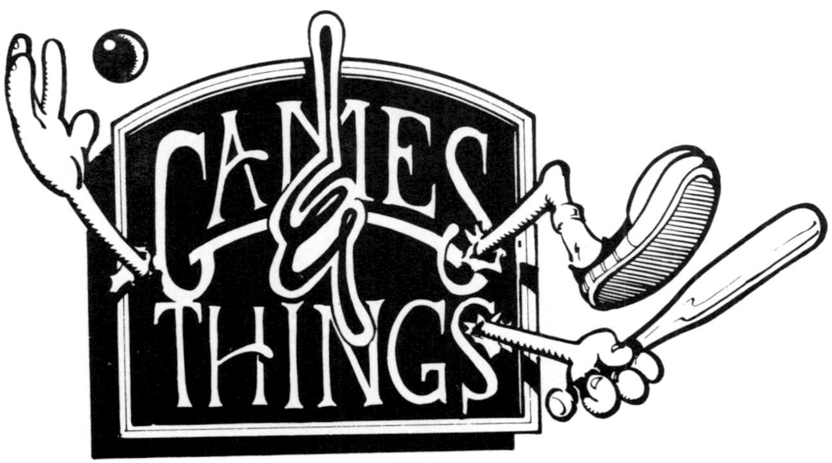
GAMES & THINGS

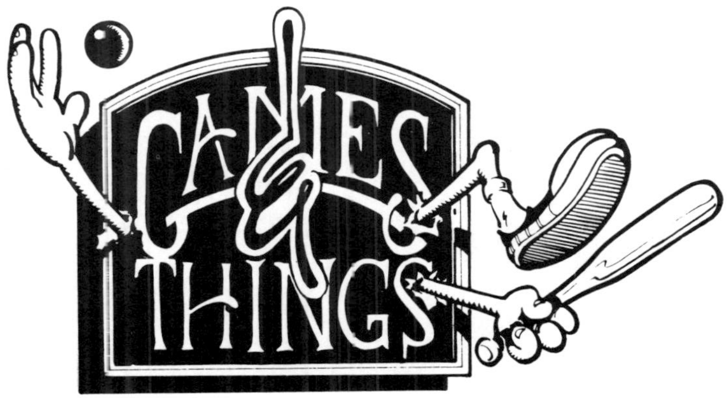
GAMES & THINGS

SEE YA
AT
CAMP!

Summer Fun!

CAMP

CAMP

CAMP

CAMP

WAH!
ICE CREAM SOCIAL

WAH!
ICE CREAM SOCIAL

POOL PARTY

POOL PARTY

GET ON THE BUS

BEACH TRIP!

BEACH TRIP!

MISCELLANEOUS

1.

2.

3.

4.

5.

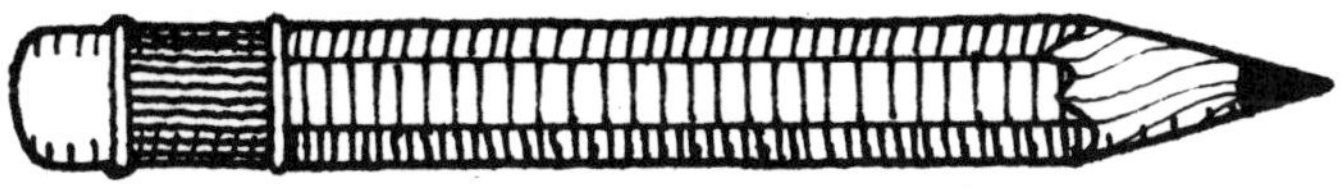

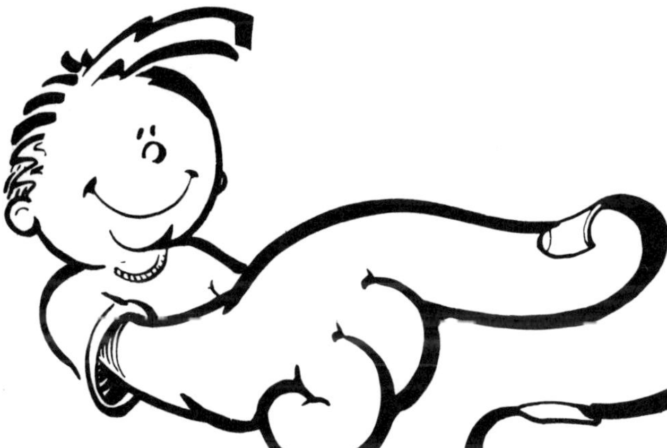

FUN!

FUN!

CRAYON

12
9
3
6

12
9
3
6

BIBLE
BIBLE

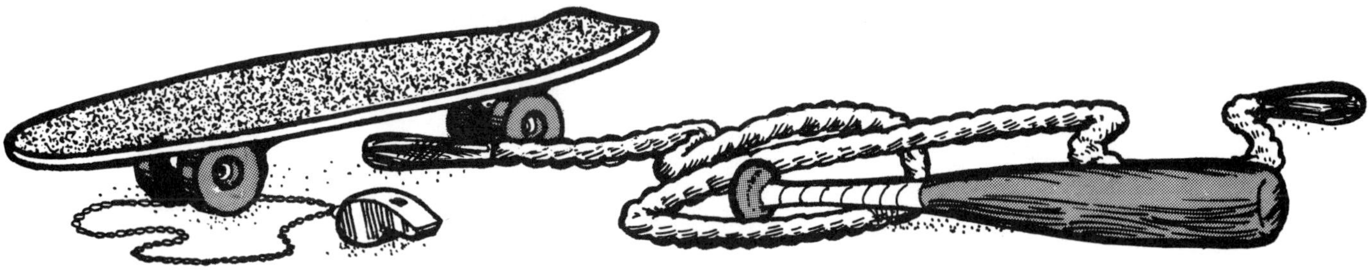

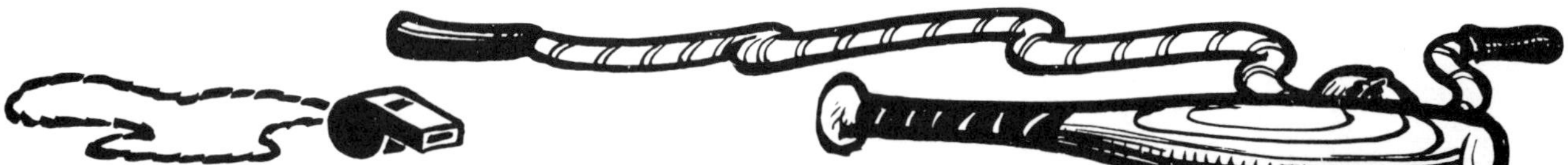

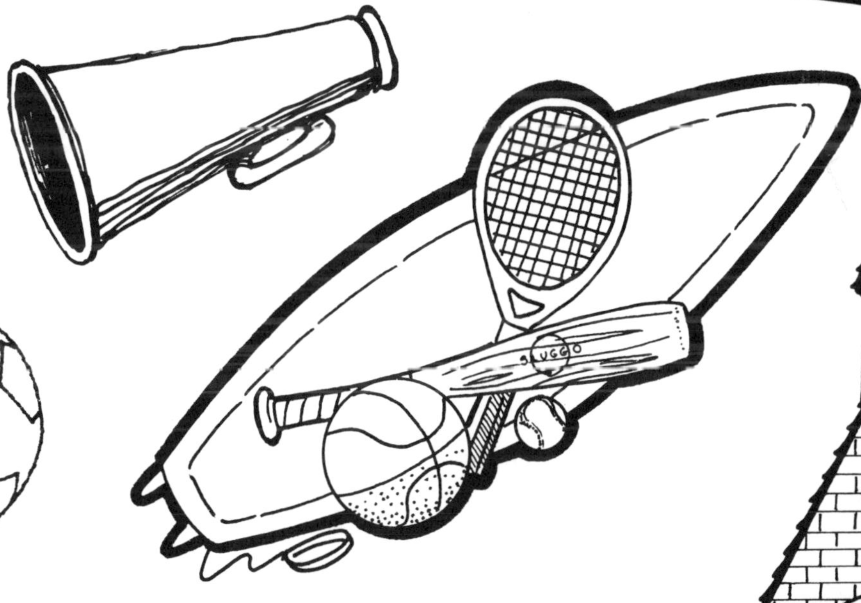

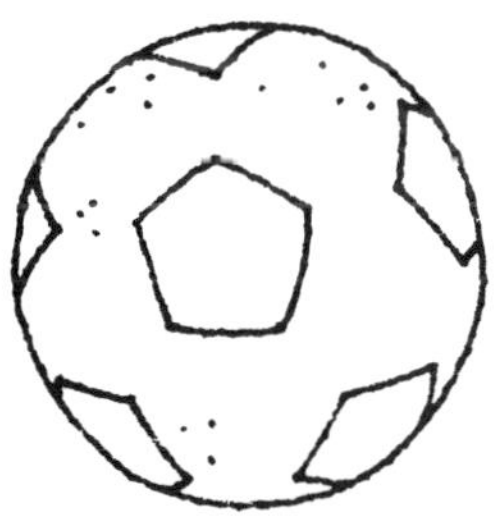

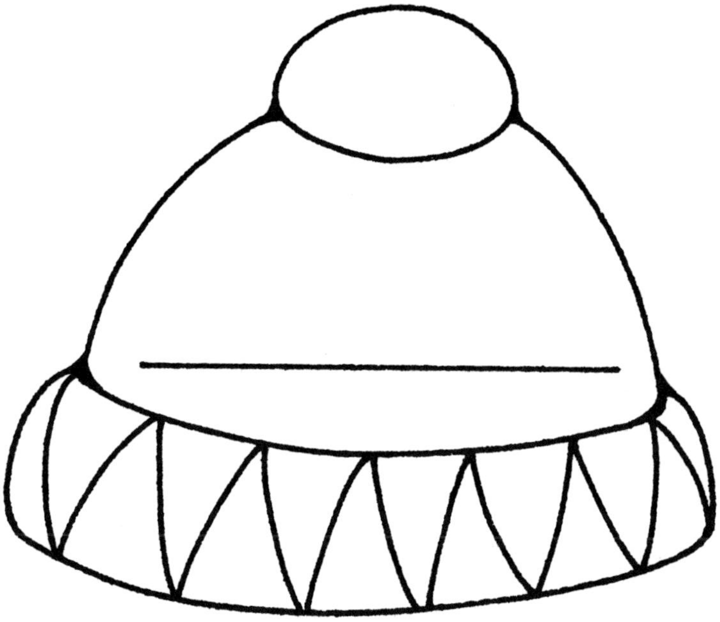

Name tags

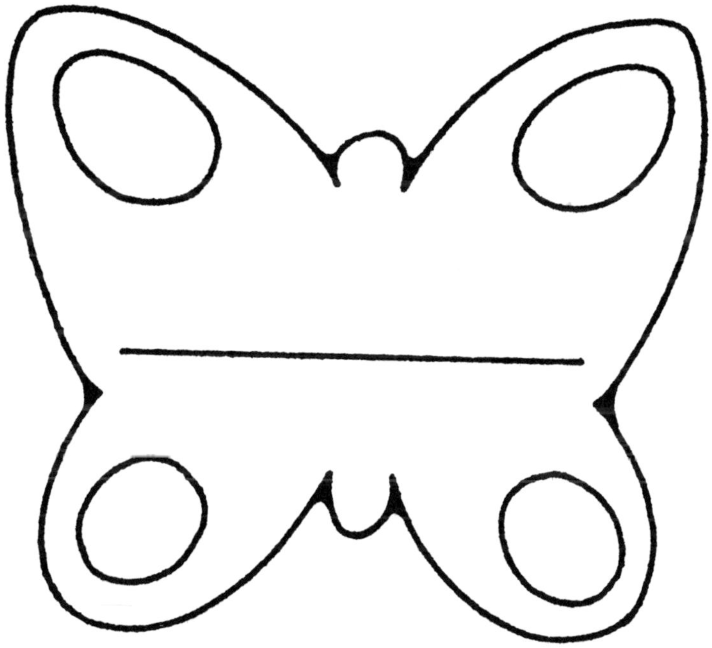

____
(date)

Pay to the order of ______________________________

I will ______________________________________.

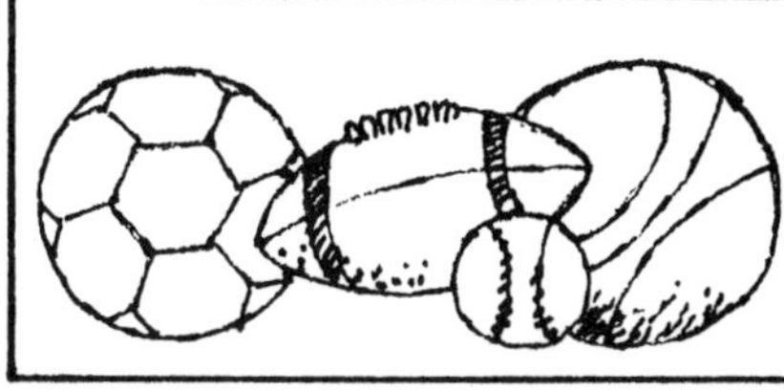

____
(name)

Name tags

Name tag

BORDERS

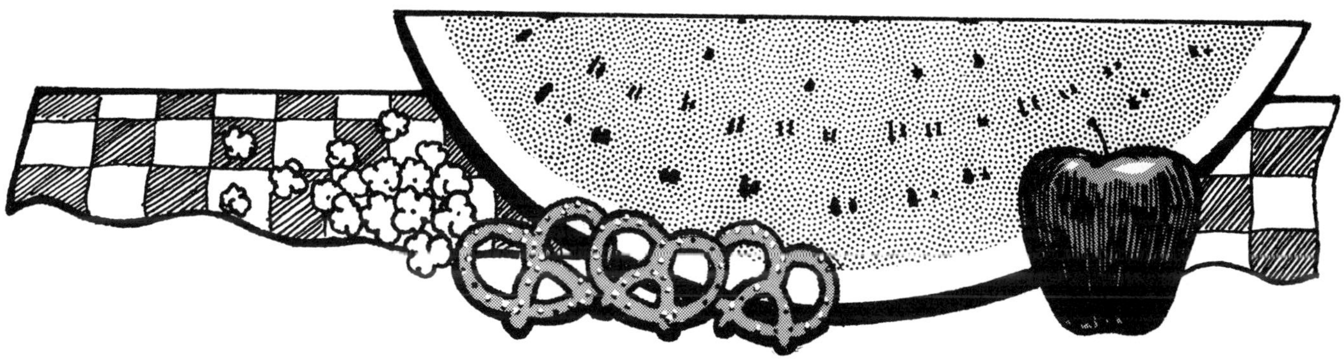

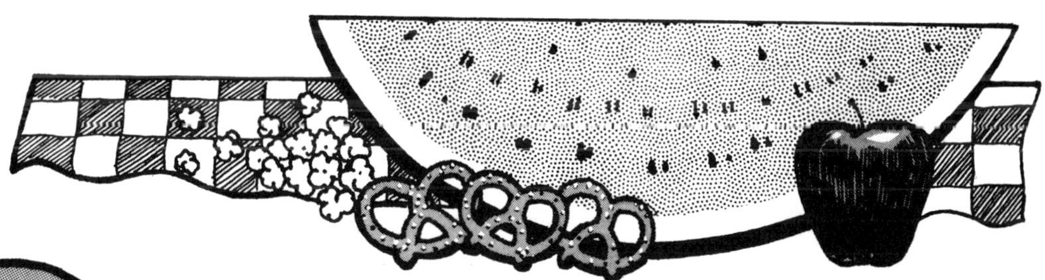

Jesu
GLUE

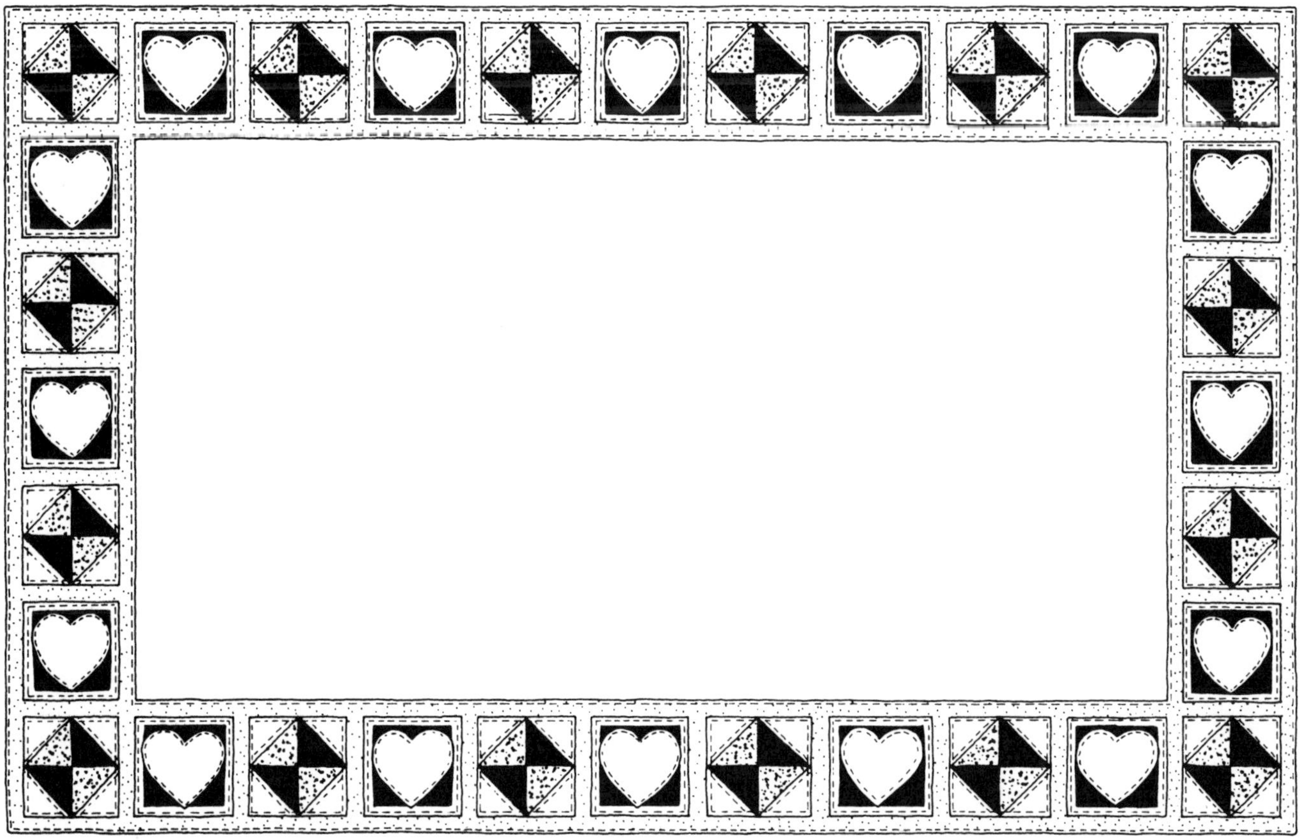

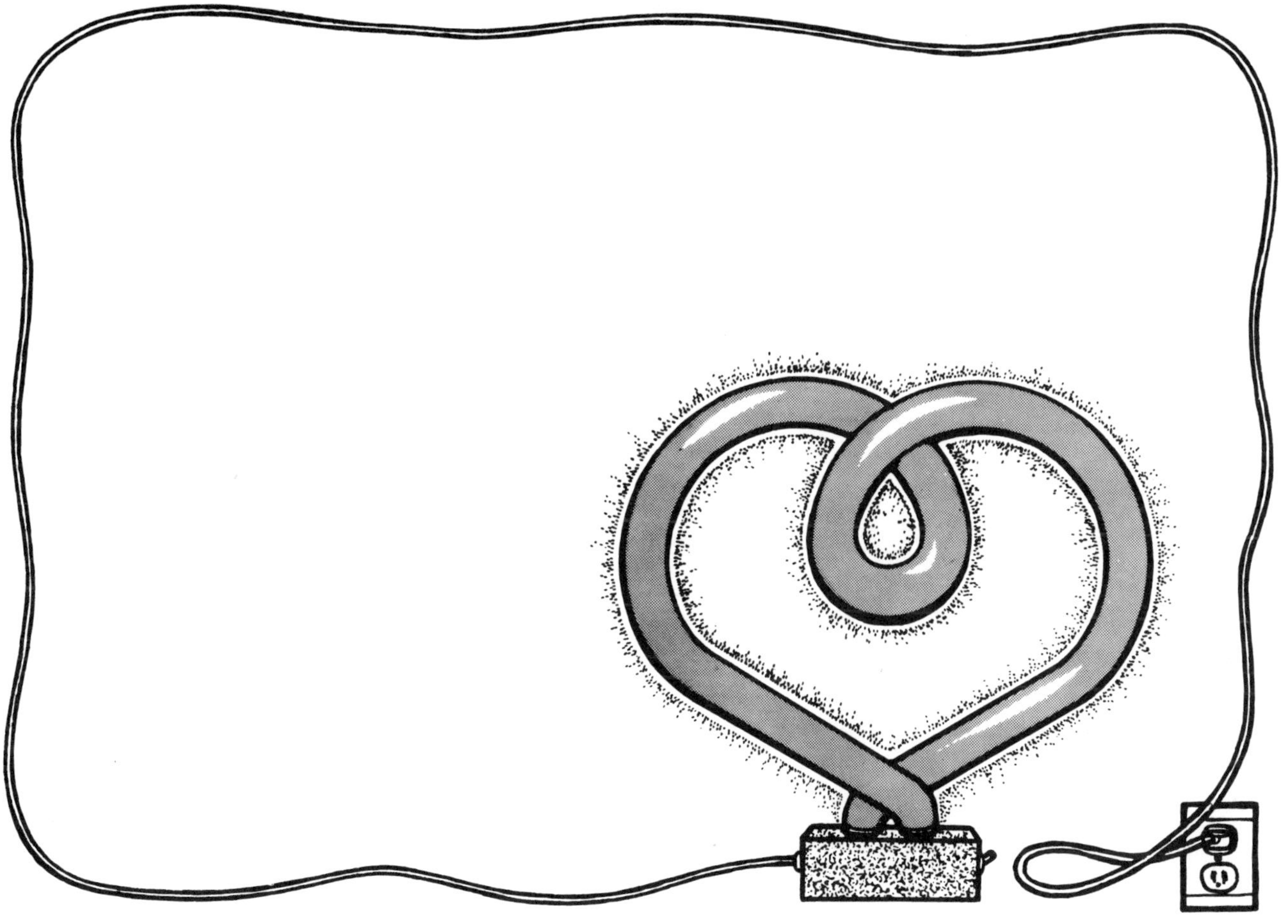

TV

Adventure Day
ADVENTURE DAY
Beach Party

Adventure Day Beach Party Beach Party

BIRTHDAY PARTY FOR JESUS CAMP

Birthday Party for Jesus Camp

Birthday Party for Jesus Camp

CHILDREN'S MINISTRIES CALENDAR

Children's Ministries Calendar

Children's Ministries Calendar

CHILDREN'S MUSICAL DAY CAMP

Children's Musical Day Camp

Children's Musical Day Camp

Children's Choir Concert for Kids

Children's Choir Concert for Kids

CHILDREN'S CHOIR CONCERT FOR KIDS

Dear Parents, Dear Teacher,

Dear Parents,

Dear Teacher,

DEAR PARENTS,

DEAR TEACHER,

CAMP-OUT

Fall Festival

Camp-out

Fall Festival

CAMP-OUT

FALL FESTIVAL

FAMILY PICNIC

Family Fun Fair

Family Camp

Family Fun Fair

Family Potluck

FAMILY FUN FAIR

FAMILY CAMP

FAMILY PICNIC

FAMILY CAMP

FAMILY PICNIC

FAMILY POTLUCK

FAMILY POTLUCK

Father/Daughter

Father/Son

FATHER/DAUGHTER

FATHER/SON

Father/Daughter

Father/Son

Film Night

Games

Film Night

Games

FILM NIGHT

GAMES

Handbook Good News Help Wanted

Handbook Good News Help Wanted

HANDBOOK GOOD NEWS HELP WANTED

Kids Are Special People! Kids' Concert

Kids Are Special People!

Kids' Concert KIDS' DAY

KIDS ARE SPECIAL PEOPLE! KIDS' CONCERT

Kids in Action Kids' Day Listen Up

Kids in Action Kids' Day Listen Up

KIDS IN ACTION LISTEN UP

Kids' Missions Conference Missions Month

Kids' Missions Conference Missions Month

KIDS' MISSIONS CONFERENCE MISSIONS MONTH

Mark Your Calendar Missions Week

Mark Your Calendar Missions Week

MARK YOUR CALENDAR MISSIONS WEEK

Mother/Daughter Special Mother/Son Event

Mother/Daughter Special
Mother/Son Event MOTHER/SON EVENT
MOTHER/DAUGHTER SPECIAL

Nursery News Pancake Breakfast Please Note

Nursery News Pancake Breakfast Please Note

NURSERY NEWS PANCAKE BREAKFAST PLEASE NOTE

Parents' Meeting Planning Meeting

Parents' Meeting Planning Meeting

PARENTS' MEETING PLANNING MEETING

Prime Time for Kids Promotion Sunday

Prime Time for Kids Promotion Sunday

PRIME TIME FOR KIDS PROMOTION SUNDAY

Registration Save This Date Schedule

Registration Save This Date Schedule

REGISTRATION SAVE THIS DATE SCHEDULE

Sign Up Now! Skating Party Special Event

Sign Up Now! Skating Party Special Event

SIGN UP NOW! SKATING PARTY SPECIAL EVENT

Soccer Camp Summer Camp Staff News

Soccer Camp Summer Camp Staff News

SOCCER CAMP SUMMER CAMP STAFF NEWS

Sunday School Swimming Party

Sunday School Swimming Party

SUNDAY SCHOOL SWIMMING PARTY

Teacher News Teachers Are Special People!

Teacher News Teachers Are Special People!

Teacher News Teachers Are Special People!

Teachers' Bible Study Teachers' Meeting

Teachers' Bible Study Teachers' Meeting

Thanks for Coming! Thank You!

Thanks for Coming! Thank You!

THANKS FOR COMING! THANK YOU!

Thanks for your help! Thanks for your help!

Welcome to our Sunday School!

Welcome to our Sunday School!

WELCOME TO OUR SUNDAY SCHOOL!

You Are Invited You Are Invited YOU'RE #1

You're #1 You're #1 You Are Invited

ZOO TRIP Zoo Trip Zoo Trip

Fall Winter Spring Summer

Babies Junior Workshop

Babies Junior Workshop

BABIES JUNIOR WORKSHOP

Toddlers Preschool Primary Middler

Toddlers Preschool Primary Middler

TODDLERS PRESCHOOL PRIMARY MIDDLER

January
FEBRUARY
march
April
MAY
JUNE
JULY
AUGUST
September
MATH
OCTOBER
NOVEMBER
December

COMING SOON:

COMING SOON:

COMING SOON:

Summer Specials—

Summer Specials—

Summer Specials—

PUT THIS ON YOUR CALENDAR

NEXT SUNDAY:

NEXT SUNDAY:

PUT THIS ON YOUR CALENDAR

COMING ☆ UP...

COMING ☆ UP...

COMING ☆ UP...

COMING ☆ UP...

1. 2. 3. 4. 5.

1. 2. 3. 4. 5.

1. 2. 3. 4. 5.

EVERY SUNDAY MORNING

This Month:

EVERY SUNDAY MORNING

This Month:

This Month:

EVERY SUNDAY MORNING

Sign up!

Sign up!

Join Us!

COMING SOON:

Join Us!

DON'T FORGET TO REMEMBER!

DON'T FORGET TO REMEMBER!